I Like to Collect

Michael Wagner

Contents

We Collect!

Look at all these things.
We like to collect them.

2

It is fun to collect things!

3

Cars

I am Mark.
I collect cars.

I have lots of fast cars!

These cars are made of metal.

5

Marbles

I am Ben.
I collect marbles.

I have little marbles.
I have big marbles.

These marbles are made of glass.

Ponies

I am Alisha.
I collect ponies.

My ponies have long hair.
I like my ponies a lot!

These ponies
are made
of plastic.

Cards

I am Beth.
I collect cards.

I swap cards with Adam.
Then I get cards that I like!

These cards are made of paper.

Toys

I am Adam.
I collect these toys.

Beth collects the toys too.
We like to swap.
It is lots of fun!

These toys are made of plastic.

Lots of Things

There are lots of things to collect.
What do you like best?

Toy Chart

made of glass	made of metal	made of paper	made of plastic	made of plastic